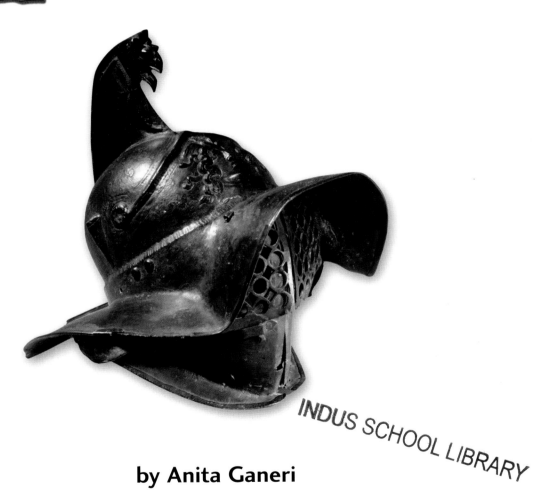

by Anita Ganeri

Consultant: Thorsten Opper

GARETH**STEVENS**

PUBLISHING

A WRC Media Company

Please visit our web site at: www.garethstevens.com
For a free color catalog describing Gareth Stevens Publishing's
list of high-quality books and multimedia programs, call
1-800-542-2595 (USA) or 1-800-387-3178 (Canada).
Gareth Stevens Publishing's fax: (414) 332-3567.

Library of Congress Cataloging-in-Publication Data

Ganeri, Anita, 1961-
    Gladiators and ancient Rome / Anita Ganeri.
        p. cm. — (A first look at history)
    ISBN 0-8368-4525-0 (lib. bdg.)
    1. Rome—Social life and customs—Juvenile literature.
2. Gladiators—Juvenile literature. I. Title. II. Series.
DG78.G38   2005
937—dc22   2004059188

This edition first published in 2005 by
Gareth Stevens Publishing
A WRC Media Company
330 West Olive Street, Suite 100
Milwaukee, Wisconsin 53212 USA

This U.S. edition copyright © 2005 by Gareth Stevens, Inc.
Original edition copyright © 2004 by ticktock Entertainment Ltd.
First published in Great Britain in 2005 by ticktock Media Ltd.,
Unit 2, Orchard Business Centre, North Farm Road, Tunbridge
Wells, Kent, TN2 3XF, United Kingdom.

Gareth Stevens series editor: Dorothy L. Gibbs
Gareth Stevens art direction: Tammy West

Picture credits (t=top, b=bottom, c=center, l=left, r=right)
Alamy: 4-5b. Album-online: 6-7, 10-11. Ancient Art and Architecture:
21cr. Art Archive: 9tl, 11l, 11br, 12, 14, 15tl, 15tr, 16 (both), 18, 22,
23 (all). Bridgeman Art Library: 17tr. British Museum: 11tr, 15br,
17bl, 17br, 19br. Corbis: 5tr, 7l, 7br, 9br. Martin Coulbert: 20-21.
Heritage Image Partnership: 19tr. PHOTOS12: 1, 2-3, 7tr, 8-9.
Ticktock: 4tl, 4bl, 5tl, 5br, 9tr, 9cr, 13 (all), 15bl, 18-19tl, 19bl,
21tl, 21tr, 21br. Werner Forman: 17tl.

Printed in the United States of America

1 2 3 4 5 6 7 8 9 09 08 07 06 05

Contents

Words in the glossary are printed in **boldface** type the first time they appear in the text.

The Roman Empire

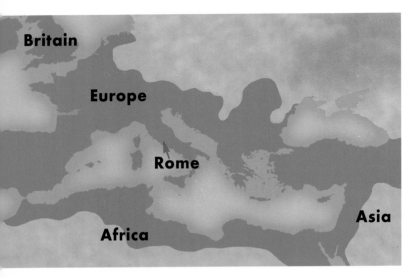

Today, Rome is the capital city of Italy, but two thousand years ago, Rome was the center of a great and powerful **empire**.

The green areas on this map show the Roman Empire two thousand years ago.

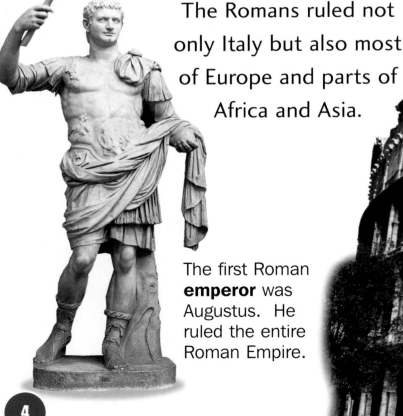

The Romans ruled not only Italy but also most of Europe and parts of Africa and Asia.

The first Roman **emperor** was Augustus. He ruled the entire Roman Empire.

Rome was the biggest city in the empire. About one million people lived there.

The Forum, in Rome, was once a **marketplace**. It was surrounded by temples and government buildings. Now, only **ruins** remain.

Gladiator fights in Rome were held at the Colosseum. This huge building could seat fifty thousand people!

Roman Artifacts

People today know a lot about **ancient** Rome because of the **artifacts** the Romans left behind.

This **mosaic** is a picture of a Roman gladiator.

Ancient Roman coins can still be found all over the area that was once the Roman Empire.

Gladiators

On festival days, the Romans liked to go out and have fun. They especially enjoyed watching gladiator fights.

These battles to the death seem cruel to most people today, but the Romans loved them!

A scene from the movie *Gladiator*.

Some historians believe the crowd decided what happened to the loser at the end of a gladiator fight. A stabbing sign with the thumb toward the throat meant the loser should be killed. A raised right arm with a finger pointed in the air meant the loser should live.

A helmet protected the gladiator's head — but the gladiator could not see very well!

There were different kinds of gladiators. A retiarius fought with a trident and a net. A secutor fought with a short sword and a shield.

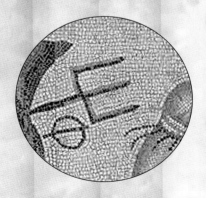

A trident was a long spear with three sharp spikes at one end. It was used for stabbing.

Gladiator Schools

Most gladiators were **slaves**, **criminals**, or prisoners of war. There were even some women gladiators. To become gladiators, they went to special schools where they were trained to fight.

The gladiator trainer was called a magister. The magister was an old gladiator whose fighting days were over. Magisters were tough and very strict.

Every day, gladiators had to do exercises with weights to build up their muscles. They also practiced fighting with heavy, wooden training swords.

A scene from the movie *Gladiator*.

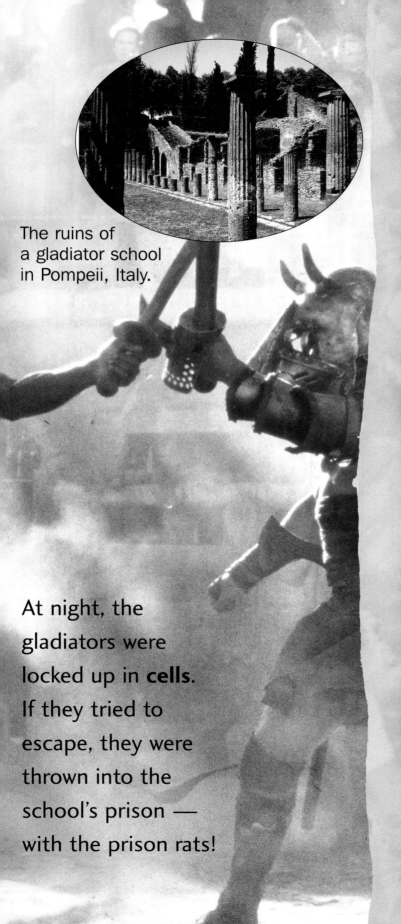

The ruins of a gladiator school in Pompeii, Italy.

At night, the gladiators were locked up in **cells**. If they tried to escape, they were thrown into the school's prison — with the prison rats!

Roman Artifacts

The prize given to a winning gladiator was usually money and a palm branch.

Some gladiators won a **laurel wreath** to wear on their heads.

The greatest prize was a wooden sword called a rudis. It meant that the gladiator had won freedom!

Races and Baths

Another kind of fun for Romans was going to the **circus** to cheer on their favorite teams at the chariot races.

Chariots were small, two-wheeled carts pulled by two or four horses.

Roman charioteers from the movie *Ben Hur*.

Chariot races were fast and furious. Many chariot drivers, called charioteers, were injured or killed, but it was worth the danger to win the race. Winning charioteers became superstars!

The Roman baths at Bath, England.

Bathing was also important to Romans, and public baths were open to everyone. At the baths, people did exercises and bathed in hot and cold pools of water.

Roman Artifacts

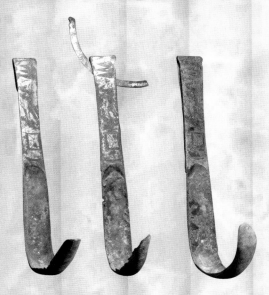

Instead of using soap to bathe, the Romans coated themselves with olive oil. They removed the oil and dirt with long, metal scrapers.

Roman vases like these often contained perfume.

11

Roman Homes

Wealthy Romans had two homes — a large house in the city and a **villa** in the countryside. Poor people in Rome lived in crowded apartment buildings.

Roman apartment buildings could be up to six stories high. They were badly built and often burned down.

Most of these buildings did not have running water, toilets, or kitchens. Poor Romans had to get their water from fountains in the streets and buy hot food from shops.

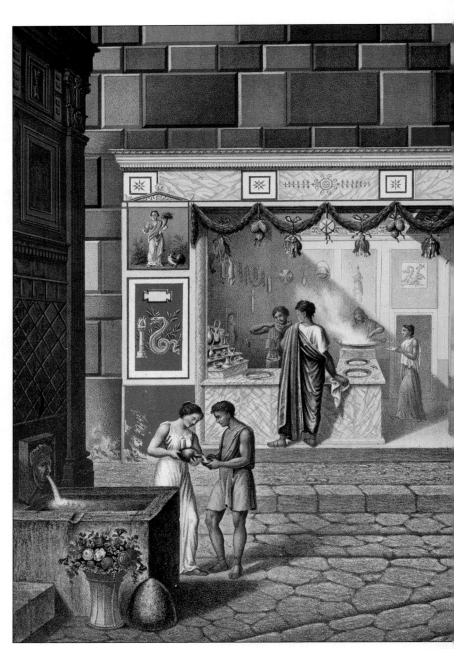

A Roman villa in Pompeii, Italy.

The houses and villas of the rich were built around outdoor **courtyards** and gardens. They had kitchens, indoor water supplies, and **central heating**.

In ancient Rome, clay or metal lamps that burned olive oil were used to light homes.

Roman Artifacts

The homes of wealthy Romans were beautifully decorated. Patterns of small tiles, called mosaics, covered the floors.

The walls of Roman houses and villas were decorated with **frescoes**.

Roman Food

Poor Romans ate simple foods, such as bread and **porridge**. Wealthy Romans often gave dinner parties where they served dishes such as stuffed **dormouse** or flamingo with **dates**!

Dinner was the main meal of the day. It began in the late afternoon. In wealthy households, people lay on couches around the table and ate with their fingers. Slaves brought food to them and took away the empty dishes.

A mosaic of Romans eating and drinking.

14

A Roman slave preparing food.

For rich Romans, slaves did all the cooking. Food was cooked over a stove that burned either wood or charcoal.

The main drink in Roman times was water or wine mixed with water. Even poor Romans drank wine. The wine was made from grapes.

Roman Artifacts

For cooking, Romans used pans made of metals such as **bronze**.

Herbs and spices helped hide the taste of foods that had **spoiled**.

This Roman cup is made of glass. Cups were also made of silver or clay.

Roman Fashion

The Romans wore simple, loose-fitting clothes so they would be comfortable in hot weather. Most of their clothes were made of linen or wool. All Romans wore strappy leather sandals to keep their feet cool.

Men wore **tunics** for working and sleeping. On special occasions, they wore long, white robes called togas. Important men wore togas that had a purple stripe.

An ancient Roman sandal.

Men wearing togas at a wedding.

Like Roman men, Roman boys also wore tunics. At age fourteen, boys were given special white togas to show that they were now grown up.

Roman women wore long dresses with tunics underneath, and young girls dressed like their mothers.

Rich or poor, Roman women wore jewelry. Many women had their ears **pierced** to wear earrings. Roman women also wore makeup. They used ashes for eye shadow.

Roman Artifacts

Wealthy Romans used combs made of **ivory**. Poor Romans used combs made of bone or wood.

The large ends of these Roman toothpicks may have been used for cleaning the ears.

School Days

Many Roman boys went to work instead of school, and girls usually stayed at home to help their mothers. Boys from rich families, however, started school when they were about six years old.

School began very early in the morning and lasted until midday. The boys learned to read, write, count, and do mathematics.

A Roman teacher with his pupils.

Romans used a pointed metal pen called a stylus to scratch letters into wax.

The Romans spoke and wrote a language called Latin. Most of the letters in the Latin alphabet were made up of straight lines, which made them easy to carve or scratch into wax or stone.

Roman numbers were called numerals. They looked like letters, such as V for 5 and C for 100. Roman numerals are still seen today on clocks and wristwatches.

Children practiced writing by scratching letters onto a wooden board that was covered with wax. Old wax could be scraped off the board and a new layer added.

Army Life

The Roman army was the biggest and the best in the ancient world. It conquered new lands, guarded the empire's **borders**, and kept the peace. Men stayed in the army for twenty to twenty-five years.

Ordinary Roman soldiers were called legionaries. Their lives were hard and dangerous. Besides fighting battles, they had to march long distances across the empire, carrying heavy **weapons** and supplies.

Legionaries carried shields and sharply pointed **javelins** called pilums.

Modern-day actors dressed as Roman legionaries.

The ruins of the Vindolanda Roman fort, in England.

When legionaries stayed in one place for a long time, they built a stone fort to live in.

Roman soldiers wore protective metal helmets.

Some Roman soldiers used a short sword called a gladius. "Gladiator" comes from the name of this sword.

A razor-sharp dagger called a pugio had a deadly, double-edged blade.

Gods and Temples

The people of ancient Rome worshiped many different gods and goddesses. The Romans built grand temples in honor of their gods. Each temple was special to a god or goddess, and a statue of that god stood inside.

The Romans believed that a temple was a god's home. They would go inside the temple to pray to the god. Sometimes, they left **offerings** for the god outside the temple.

The ruins of a temple to Bacchus, the Roman god of wine.

Women praying to a statue
of the goddess Venus.

Romans also worshiped their gods at home. Every home had a small **shrine**. Roman families prayed every day to the gods who looked after their homes, such as Vesta, the goddess of the hearth, or fireplace.

Roman Gods

Venus was the goddess of love. She was very beautiful.

Jupiter was the king of the gods and the god of thunder and lightning.

Mars was the god of war. The month of March is named after him.

Glossary

ancient: from a time early in history

artifacts: items, such as tools and decorative objects, made by people

borders: the edges, or boundaries, of a country or territory

bronze: a mixture of copper and tin

cells: very small rooms

central heating: a way of heating an entire building from inside the building

circus: a circular track with seats around it that was used for chariot races and other public entertainment

courtyards: parklike areas surrounded by the walls of one or more buildings

criminals: people who break laws

dates: the sweet fruits of palm trees

dormouse: an animal that is a lot like both a mouse and a squirrel

emperor: the ruler of an empire

empire: a large group of lands ruled by one powerful leader

frescoes: pictures painted on wet plaster walls

gladiator: a person who, in ancient Rome, fought deadly battles with an opponent to entertain the public

ivory: the hard, creamy white material that elephant tusks are made of

javelins: lightweight, long-handled spears for long-distance throwing

laurel wreath: a circular branch of leaves from a laurel tree, which is a small evergreen; a symbol of victory

marketplace: an open area where many different kinds of goods are sold

mosaic: a picture made out of small stones or bits of broken tiles or glass

offerings: gifts from people to gods

pierced: made a small hole, using a thin tool with a sharp point

porridge: a grain, such as oatmeal, cooked in boiling water until it thickens

ruins: the remains of buildings damaged by disasters, war, or weather

shrine: a special place devoted to a god or some other object of worship

slaves: people who are sold to work as servants

spoiled: became bad or unsafe to eat

tunics: long shirts that look like sleeveless dresses

villa: a large house with a lot of yard and garden space

wealthy: having a lot of money and valuable possessions

weapons: dangerous objects used to kill or seriously injure others